FELTON HAWKINS

INCREASE!

SELF-VALUE
PERSONAL EQUITY
LEADERSHIP IQ

Put Your Business Mindset in Discovery Mode and Unfold the Intrinsic Details of Leadership Development

Increase! Self-Value, Personal Equity, Leadership IQ: Put Your Business Mastery Mindset in Discovery Mode and Unfold the Intrinsic Details of Leadership Development

This book can be ordered in bulk for organizations and is supported by a comprehensive workbook that is made available exclusively in live workshop settings facilitated by the author. Please contact us at hawkinssolutions.org to get more information on having Felton Hawkins facilitate a workshop for your corporate, private, or non-profit organizations.

Paperback ISBN: xxxxxxxxxxxxx

Ebook ISBN: xxxxxxxxxxxxx

LCCN Number: xxxxxxxxxx

INCREASE!

SELF-VALUE, PERSONAL EQUITY, LEADERSHIP IQ - HOW TO PUT YOUR BUSINESS MINDSET IN DISCOVERY MODE AND UNFOLD THE INTRINSIC DETAILS OF LEADERSHIP DEVELOPMENT

FELTON HAWKINS

For my Family

ACKNOWLEDGMENTS

I would like to take the time to acknowledge all of the wonderful people that worked so hard to help me produce this book. Thank you to my wife Jasanta who is always allowing me to bounce my ideas off of her and giving me great feedback; Janelle who works all the time to make my work legible and readable. I can't say enough about Kimberly Millionaire who guides me through the process, always being supportive and sharing her expertise with me when it comes to the publishing of my works. Thank you to all of you who support and pray for me always. Without you, I would have never gotten this and other projects off of the grown. Words will never be able to express my gratitude. Believe me, it takes a whole lot of great people to make me look good. Thank You!

CONTENTS

PREFACE

As baby boomers are leaving the workforce in the droves for retirement, many organizations find themselves under pressure to replace the knowledge, experience, and expertise that go with them. This void leaves them competing for the best and brightest talent available and looking for employees who possess the education and skills to fill these vacated positions. While most organizations are motivated to ensure employees are properly trained, they provide extra incentives such as specialized training, access to workshops, and networking and mentoring opportunities, etc. they struggle to acquire individuals who have the work ethic, mindset, and core attitudes that will continue their success. They often look to promote internally, yet it remains, they still are unable to find the talented candidates they seek although they have a sea of employees to choose from. So what can you do?

The organization must give you information to help you understand what alignment with the company looks like. The employee must then know that they possess the will, mindset, and attitude to adjust themselves properly to align themselves with the organization. Every employee should see themselves as a brand and take the proactively increasing their equity and leadership IQ. My goal is to help you think in revolutionary ways about who you are beyond just an employee. I challenge you to look deep, eliminate excuses, and forge ahead with the insight and confidence you need to succeed in life. Remove the glass ceiling, break barriers, and embrace opportunities that await you because you have the equity it takes.

1

EQUITY ISSUES IN CULTURE OF ORGANIZATIONS

Workplace equity is the result of a proactive commitment to increase one's value within the organization while understanding that this is key in adding or raising the value of the overall organization. For a person to reach the point of equity, they must first realize that their mindset must move from the perspective of loss (i.e., money loss, time loss). You can never accomplish ownership thinking, 'I have to lose these essential things to survive in this organization.' Employees at all levels, from management to average worker, must think in terms of the law of reciprocity. This law means that sometimes investments may appear to be lost. In reality, it is the intent to grow with the understanding that investments are unseen values growing and manifesting with more increased value and benefit in a time somewhere in the future. Most people never invest because they have not overcome the emotional feeling of loss. Many times, this feeling comes from a status of lack based on the employee's belief that he or she, from the beginning, is limited. They, out of severe need, can only look to receive with very little to give, if anything. They believe they are privileged to obtain but are aware of very little that they have to invest.

Charles was a great kid with a bright future with nothing to lose and everything to gain. He was proud to be the first in his immediate family to attend college, pursuing a degree in entrepreneurship. During his college years, Charles was too immature to stay on task, and lacked the discipline needed to successfully maneuver through his course work. Oftentimes he prioritized partying over studying, which resulted in him being an average student at best. Charles disappointed himself and his family when instead of achieving his degree in the intended four years, he had to enroll in two additional semesters to complete his studies.

"I've learned my lesson," he thought after pulling himself from his self-created strop. Taking on a menial job, he moved off campus and into a small apartment with a

friend who'd been been able to graduate on time. Although he'd vowed to completely focus on his schoolwork, his old habits were hard to escape. He felt that he was in the best years of his adult life, and thought it would be a shame not to enjoy himself. After all, in his mind, he'd be slaving away at a job for the rest of his life... or at least until he'd start his own business. With that mentality, he did little to cut back on his social life, but somehow he'd met the requirements to culminate his studies and finally walk across the stage celebrating a significant milestone.

Filled with pride and armed with his education, he sought out to establish a career, choosing to apply at the same apprentice school as his roommate. He'd watch him not only earn a nice salary, but obtain a promotion in just a year's time. Charles was confined that with a degree from the same university, he could easily do the same. He was elated when just a few weeks later he'd received the acceptance letter.

"Good!" he huffed. "They can start helping me pay these student loans." He could hardly hide his excitement as he shared the news with his roommate, who congratulated, but just as quickly warned him.

"It's a great opportunity for sure," he'd started; "but listen. This is not like college."

"What you do you mean; it's school," Charles shrugged dismissively.

"I mean it requires some tedious hours of both studying and working. It's not the same environment and culture as just goofing off on campus, thinking they owe you something because you've paid your tuition. It's a completely different culture. You're going to have to work."

His words stung a bit, but Charles quickly shook it off. In his mind this was a perfect way for him use his degree to easily accelerate up the ladder of success with quick promotions, and get himself on a solid path to achieving his financial goals. As far as he was concerned, he already had a leg-up on any worker they'd bring in with a high school education. He'd paid good money for his degree and his plan was to let it work for him.

To build personal equity you must understand that what you possess can be incorporated and developed to improve your value beyond average or mediocre coworkers.

This equity can be accomplished beyond being intelligent, gifted, and knowledgeable. Take inventory of yourself. What is it you have that either you're not using or have not yet had the opportunity to use. Maybe it could be that you're a great organizer, event planner, or you have excellent customer service skills. Perhaps you're good at art, can sing, or skilled at playing an instrument. The challenge here in realizing personal equity is to resist putting these great qualities on the shelf because your equity is not being used in the normal operations of a nine-to-five job.

Nobody knows half of what they need to realize about who you are and what you possess that has value and adds value to others who will benefit from them in time to come. For example, your department has planned a big annual event where you will have the ability to design and use decorations that makes the event elegant and impressive. You overhear your boss saying, 'we need someone who can make this happen, do a great job and avoid breaking the budget.' This could be a great time to use your equity; raise your hand to assure him that you can knock it out of the box. Ask your boss for the chance to show off your stuff.

Can you imagine if you took on that task, even though the project is not directly related to your job, how it would show your extended value beyond your job description? How would this raise the awareness of those around you? How would this connect you to more people who are impressed by your initiative and willingness to step up and make a difference? Do you think that your name will be forgotten that you won't have a special place in the hearts of those who can help you? Consider that when they are looking for someone to promote, head up a new department, or even create a job that is needed, you could fill the position. I know too many people who limit themselves to just one thing they do. Although they do it well, they tend to get tunnel vision and take for granted their other gifts and skills. If they would only recognize how important these other precious gifts are and just look for ways to incorporate them into organizations for which they are already a part of. Increasing your personal equity can be executed by implementing an idea for a new way to include a system, suggesting a better way to do a job that saves the company thousands of dollars ore redefining processes that may be outdated and need restructuring, just to name a few.

> "Even if you are not considered an entrepreneur, you should think more like one in terms of your brand.

Also, if you work for an organization, think about how you can build your brand in a way that best reflects who you are and exposes your value to others beyond just a set of job skills. This unorthodox way of thinking could open you up to a whole new world. Entrepreneurs are usually more open to doing the extra thing, working the extra hours, and being creative to help their business thrive. It would be great if you could work like you love your job but think like an entrepreneur. In either scenario, you are working for yourself, family, and the dreams and goals that you all share.

Working in organizations, learning systems, and engaging in processes should be seen as training, an opportunity to know what you are made of. When our attitude is to grow and become better in an organization, it will help you understand your weaknesses and strengths. This will cause you to take a look in the mirror and ask yourself some very probing questions that help raise your level of expectation about the possibilities that are before you. I have heard many people boldly proclaim that they do not want a promotion, they are not willing to put more time into their career, they are not going back to school, they don't want more responsibility, they don't want to be a company man. What they are saying is that somewhere along the way they have settled. They have made themselves content and have accepted whatever it will be at their current status. Everyone has a right to choose their limits or how far they are willing to go to have a certain level of success. However, they also have to realize, that was their choice when their options are limited, rewards are minimal, and they have given others more leverage to control their growth in life. We all have choices, and no one has the right to question the choices you make for your own life but in turn, recognize that it is never because of the choices someone else made, only you have that privilege and power.

Key Takeaways

2

LEADERSHIP IQ

Leadership IQ is the ability to understand how to identify the gifts, skills, and assets that one possesses and how they can effectively work in a system that will advance their growth and equity, as well as the organization. Many people suffer from low leadership IQ because they don't know or recognize the wonderful things they possess that are an asset to the organization. Therefore, they don't understand how implementing these assets into the system or organization will increase their leadership IQ while at the same time, making the organization more productive and profitable.

To develop leadership IQ, one must take on a learning initiative. Many times, some barriers hinder people from being open to new ways of thinking or approaching projects and tasks. Initially, people come into organizations with their internal pictures derived from past experiences, practices, and theories. Sometimes they find it very difficult to remove old models and trust new models presented to them in a new system. Old internal models are barriers to increasing leadership IQ. Secondly, people have theories that they have accumulated about leadership and organizations. These theories are not proven accurate or applicable to the context of the organization where they are being applied.

> “People who will increase in leadership IQ must be willing to dismiss old theories for the sake of learning what works in the context of the system for which they are engaging.

Thirdly, people must be willing to dismiss assumptions and expectations that may not be beneficial in a system. They must remove those assumptions and embrace, with clarity, systems in organizations with valid information. Increased leadership IQ requires that members of the organization must be willing to challenge their own beliefs consistently. They should not fear that their opinions or assumptions from the past are obsolete or outdated. People who refuse to do this will not grow and will become stuck in old paradigms that will not serve them well in their desire to have upward mobility in the organization. They must be intentional about learning everything they can learn not only specific to their task but from the environment around them that is full of free lessons that will benefit them.

A few month's passed and Charles was less than motivated about the position for which he'd once been ecstatic in taking. Things weren't moving as quickly as he'd hoped, although he had shown up everyday on time and studied enough to make acceptable scores his varied assessments. He'd tried building rapport with academic advisor and a couple of the most skilled journeyman, but they were hardly impressed with his meaningless conversation, which confused Charles. He'd always been able to use his wit, charm and vocabulary to set himself apart, but was stunned to realize how ineffective he'd been at his first performance review. His advisor provided recommendations for improvement but Charles' disappointment would not allow him to embrace the feedback. Instead of applying this information he mentally discarded it, convincing himself that the feedback was premised on the advisor's personal feelings.

Developing leadership IQ does not cost anything, but the rewards are abundant. Low self-worth personnel only see the task in front of them. They barely master their mission, have no interest in learning it, and certainly don't care about what anyone else is doing. This approach is very limiting and depreciates their value to the organization. In contrast, high leadership IQ personnel think differently. They ask the right question: What can I learn today from the experience, environment, and people that I am fortunate to work with? They learn from everyone, even the person that they see as unfavorable, substandard, and even unnecessary. They observe others; they ask questions, love getting new information, and all the while, they are increasing their IQ and value in ways that will pay big dividends down the road. They will learn the essential functions of those around them so that in times of crisis they can do other jobs, sometimes as well as them. People who want to increase leadership IQ take free classes.

In many cases, the organization or company offers free courses to employees who desire to take advantage of them. Low IQ employees don't see the value of wasting time going to classes if they are not getting paid for them. Their attitude is, 'if I'm not going to be paid to go, then forget it,' they don't see the courses as a benefit of value offered to them to raise their equity and increase their leadership IQ. On the other hand, people who understand their value jump at the chance to take a class, they value free courses, and they look to advance themselves through courses further that the organization will reimburse them for if their grades are passing.

Key Takeaways

3

LOOK BEFORE YOU LEAP

It is imperative for those who desire to work and be productive in a particular environment to increase equity and leadership IQ. To take a proactive role in understanding how you can truly excel in this organization, you must interview your employees using levels. Interviews operate on two levels:

- The expectation of the company's criteria by which they consider prime candidates for their organization
- Particular assessments that are specific to their needs; however, this should be a 2-way street.

Employees should ask potential employers essential questions about the expectations they have. How can the organization help you meet your goals? What do they offer in the way of incentives? What are the opportunities that may exist for upward mobility? Is there continued learning or educational benefits? Is there room for flexibility? How do they deal with seniority? Are there opportunities for the areas of interest that may arise?

These and many more questions show employers that you interested, which goes far beyond the amount of money you desire to make. It would serve you well to become somewhat of a student of the organization where you intend to interview. Research may reveal to you that this company is not one that will align with your expectations and give you the support you need to be great. For those who say, 'Look, I just need a job, something is better than nothing,' and while that may be true, you owe it to yourself and your employer to give your very best, apply yourself and grow. You never know how this experience will help you immensely in the next segment of your career. Realize that companies hire people who are already in alignment with their dominant values and have characteristics that match the leadership's IQ. In other words, you should know them like the back of your hand before you approach the interview. You should know as much about their training, how it's conducted and does the training tie into your strengths and weaknesses. The more you know, the more you can prepare yourself to focus and do well throughout the training process.

> Look for role models or mentors, not just managers and supervisors.

Find someone that will take the time to share vital information with you, people who don't mind spending time with you, and helping outside of the 9-to-5 workday. You will find out that many people love and enjoy teaching and helping others to do well. Show your superiors and co-workers that you are eager to learn. You are asked questions or given tasks not to be willing to say 'I don't know,' but 'I want to learn' and 'I'm willing to learn.'

Remember, equity is about expanding value, taking the initiative, and being a constant learner. Leadership IQ requires that those working within the organization take action to evaluate its leadership models. It is wonderful to be motivated to take on more responsibility in leadership roles. Still, before making any real efforts to attain leadership positions, employees must take it upon themselves to understand that titles don't make great leaders. Ambition without the fundamental understanding of leadership will not contribute to higher leadership IQ. More specifically, it is the ability to observe and understand the leadership styles that are dominant within the culture of the organization. Employees should look for ways to examine what leaders do that brings particular success and those that seem not to be active. While this may be the case, it is not for reasons of being critical but for learning.

How do individual leadership styles operate and function within the specific systems set in the organization? Is the leadership more top-down, or is it more rounded and based on team concepts where several people are tasked with and left to decide the direction of the departments? Would the employee prefer leading from a top-down perspective or facilitating teams? Will these teams lead the projects and take more of a hands-on position when it comes to how projects are done, timelines, budgets, or personnel? Becoming familiar with leadership theories and styles can give employees the edge in terms of being educated based on these leadership concepts.

Remember that leadership IQ is the responsibility of the employee, not necessarily the organization. Employees need to see leaders who model the practices and attitudes necessary to be a leader in the organization. This will usually require an investment on the part of the employee to volunteer and value the opportunities of the little things or extra things that raise their IQ. Participating in extracurricular activities that most leaders are involved in will give employees access and opportunities to mingle, talk with, and learn from those who can help them grow and develop.

> “So many employees miss out on the chance of promotion, growth, and development because they are not willing to go the extra mile and invest themselves for the benefit of growth.

They see these opportunities as unnecessary; they don't have time; it doesn't pay any financial gain. This is why the average company or organization is having problems with the revolving door of turnover, tardiness, lack of morale, and low production. Employees must know that with the right attitude and commitment to increasing leadership IQ and their equity, the organization will become motivated to give them new levels of opportunity. Employees should be motivated to study systems within the organization, understand how they work, and offer up solutions that will improve the policies, make them more productive, save the company money, and improve the quality of work life.

Key Takeaways

4

EMOTIONAL INTELLIGENCE AND LEADERSHIP VALUE PRACTICES

Emotional intelligence and leadership value practices are key components of personal and professional development. Let's look a little deeper into the focuses of those who are intentional about increasing personal equity and leadership IQ through emotional intelligence and leadership value practices. There are five critical components of emotional intelligence: self-awareness, self-management, self-regulation, motivation, empathy, and social skills.

Self-Awareness

Self-awareness is the ability to know one's self. Self-awareness requires your ability to be clear and candid about your strengths and weaknesses. The willingness to look deeply into your strengths and weaknesses factor into your capacity to be effective. It allows you to work on those areas that you become aware of as you develop personally and professionally.

Self-Management

Self-management is the ability to control destructive, unproductive, harmful emotions, and desires that can be overcome by having committed plans, strategies, and goals. It requires discipline to identify those plans, strategies, and goals that consistently allow you to grow. Having this desire for growth will be a constant motivating factor under challenging circumstances that you face in your growth process.

Self-Regulation

Self-regulation speaks to the fact that we will work with a diversity of people, managers, supervisors, and climates. All of these will have an impact on how you are affected based on different personalities, approaches to work production, and ever-changing environments, many of which may be challenging to deal with and sometimes are the result of a hostile work environment. How we will respond in these situations will determine our success. Our response is something we must be focused on, seeking out ways to improve our behaviors and emotions so that we function in proper and effective ways.

The fact is, you can't expect people to change, and you can't control others' attitudes and behaviors. Still, you can learn how to manage yourself in the context of these challenging circumstances and deal with people who may not be in alignment with you. The majority of people you will encounter in life at some level are emotional responders. This means that their first response to change and complicated or adverse events are emotions that emit out of their poorly managed emotions. **Everyone has feelings that factor into their behavior. People who are self-aware and intentional about how they let their feelings affect their response under pressure, crises, and challenging people, are concerns that need to be addressed. Self-regulation is about harnessing one's emotions by controlling them in a way that they do not become barriers and destructive to the person or organization as a whole.

Motivation

Motivation is essential to success in any environment. Its ability does not allow people or live events to derail a sense of consistent commitment to the purpose and goals established. Environments will influence our motivation and make it easier or more challenging to keep momentum and stay motivated. Motivation is an intrinsic source attached to vision, goals, benchmarks, and purpose that give us reason to be consistent in the face of challenges that would otherwise derail our efforts.

Empathy

Empathy is the ability to put yourself in the place of someone else in terms of how they may feel in any given scenario. The author Steven Covey says to "seek first to understand before seeking to be understood." Most of the time, the emphasis is placed on the employer being empathetic towards the employee. I believe that even though this is correct, there should be a balance. The employee should be just as empathetic as he or she expects the employer to be. A great question that addresses this is, 'If I were my supervisor, would I want to deal with me? What if I was in their position as a leader? How would I handle the pressure, time restraints, deadlines, and individual levels of responsibility?' Empathy is about all of us taking the posture, 'Do unto others as you would have them do unto you.'

Social Skills

For organizations to be active, they have to have a social contest. I see this as a community, the ability to function within a society which you have joined. It's the ability to appreciate diversity, accept differences about others, and work in harmony for similar goals and visions. There are four elements of EI. First, the ability to improve the quality of life not only as it relates to the workplace but in life as a whole. Secondly, you have an excellent opportunity to improve yourself in ways they will increase equity and leadership IQ. Thirdly, commitment and desire to become a more well-balanced person. Finally, to be the best you can be. To continue evolving in all areas of life, you can commit to the mastery of these basic concepts. Empower yourself, give yourself the benefit, believe in you, invest in you, and enjoy the journey to the top wherever that might be in your life.

Key Takeaways

5

THE BUCK STOPS WITH YOU

Companies are serious and committed to bringing on the best possible fit for the jobs that need to be fulfilled. Many times, onboarding can be as expensive as 50,000 dollars and up. These companies don't have the time and money to waste on individuals who lack the skills to match the production needs of the job. They take time to see if the skills necessary to perform the job tasks are in sync.

> Companies can't afford to have people come on board and lose money because they are ill-equipped to do the job.

With that said, most companies still lose a great deal of money because, after all the due diligence, the person hired does not make it through the probation period. It is in the best interest of the company to invest in the workforce that it employs to ensure the probability needed to stay in business and outlast the stiff competition that is in the market place.

According to Dess, Lumkin, and Eiser, "...as we have noted, the first step in the process of building superior human capital is input control: attracting and selecting the right person. Many human resource professionals still approach employee selection from a lock and key mentality – that is, a fit key job (the candidate) into a lock (the job)." After a thorough assessment of both individual and job, selections are made for the best fit. This aspect of onboarding still has significant issues because this fit does not necessarily consider the mindset of the person being hired. Dess, Lumkin, and Eisner say, "Many have questioned the precise matching approach. Instead, they argue that firms can identify top performers by focusing on key employee mindsets, attitudes, social skills, and general orientations that lead to success in nearly all jobs." The idea is, you can teach a skill set, but the consensus is to hire for attitude, train for skill. To be clear, yes, there has to be a level of expertise for skilled jobs. But an open attitude, the desire to learn, the desire to grow, and being passionate about opportunities that are provided for us is even more critical to organizations that are looking for stars.

Many organizations, including management, are suffering from a workforce that has very low self-value. They see themselves as just fortunate to have somehow landed this job rather than seeing themselves as assets, which makes the organization much better once they become a part. They, therefore, look at the organization for what they can get rather than what they can give. This mindset causes employees and management to live by the principle, 'do as little as possible and get as much as you can out of the opportunity.' Many times, the perception of low, self-valued people are imposed on the company or organization with the idea that the leadership of the organization will take advantage of them and will not reward them for the effort or losses that they take to make the organization more productive and profitable. It's impossible to raise the value of the overall organization without people in the organization who have a clear and focused idea of their value and what that looks like on all levels.

> This idea that 'I must take from the organization before they take from me,' 'I must steal from the organization because for some reason eventually they will steal from me' is a silent killer of many organizations.

This attitude is realized when people who desperately need their jobs show up late, are delayed in accomplishing tasks and meeting deadlines, are consistently absent, leave early, have bad attitudes, disrespect their superiors, and spread discontent among fellow employees. It is amazing how many employees who seem to need the job the worst also have the worst attitude about what they do. They treat the organization as though it is responsible for the status of their lives and then take out their frustration on the very entity that allows them to have at least some quality of life.

Key Takeaways

6

MISSED OPPORTUNITY. WHAT ARE YOU THINKING?

One morning as a friend and I sat at breakfast, we encountered some young men who struck up a conversation with us. I happened to ask them what was their field of work. One of the young men informed us that he once worked in the shipyard in a particular trade. With pride, he told us that he had left the shipyard where he was making a good salary with benefits and took a job working for a cab company. At this point, I was beside myself that he seemed to be proud of himself and felt that he had made a great decision. I proceeded to ask why he left this job where he could learn a trade and grow in this company. He simply told me that the security gates that surrounded the yard along with the whistle that blew to start work, go to lunch, and quit working reminded him too much of a prison camp, and because of that, he could not continue to work there.

The psychology behind his action disturbed me. But then I came to grips with the fact that in today's world smart, skilled, and talented does not make money when the way people think about the opportunities afforded them are seen as ways for others to take advantage of them, take something from them, or do them harm in some way. The result becomes catastrophic not only for the employee but for the company that is faced with hiring people who look good on paper but have no values that reinforce the character needed to succeed in the company or organization.

> "When the dollar or the check is the only way an employee can measure their value, they place themselves in continuous survival mode, lose self-value and ultimately give up on opportunities that could be the start of changing their whole life for the better.

It is a concern that many millennials, along with other generations, are victims. They are victims of low-value mentality because they have done very little to earn or prove their value through a process put in place. This process requires accountability, earning the opportunity, and pride that comes with accomplishments, the lack of which creates a false sense of entitlement, which is an opportunity to give others the power to put a value on you, determine your worth, and limit the ability to increase your value.

The underlying issues with those who desire to enter into the workforce are not readily seen. Many times, the fact that a person is gifted, educated with degrees, or has made great relationships through their network, gives them a false sense of equity. In reality, they have increased potential, which is a good thing. But they fail to increase the value which the potential they possess gives them access. The preparation that is done through acquiring education, certification, or degrees only improves the opportunities needed to enter into a process that will challenge, prove, develop, grow, and increase value or equity. There is a gap many times between the preparation for the opportunity and the process that says you value yourself, the opportunity provided to you, and the people who made the opportunity available. Preparation gives one access to an opportunity to engage in a process that is necessary to determine if the education, certifications, and gifts a person possesses will grow in value or equity that will benefit the person, company, and leadership. Many times, there is resistance put forth by a person entering the process. They want the money, they take the opportunity, but they don't like the process that makes all of that possible in the first place. The process or track that they must be placed on will not only challenge what they possess through preparation, but it will also test their ability to function under pressure. Also, it will test their ability to handle the weaknesses that are revealed and deal with the emotional intelligence necessary to get along with diverse people.

Charles eventually concluded that this career field was not for him. It proves to bring challenges to him that he was not willing at the time to embrace. Instead of staying there facing the challenges doing the hard thing, and allowing himself to grow through the process, Charles decided that the grass was greener on the other side. After four years invested, going to school, and getting a great job, he felt like he could find a better place to work. What Charles failed to realize at the time was that you could change systems, go to a different culture, but you still need a mindset that will keep you engaged in ways that education, skills cannot. Failing to take a considerable measure of responsibility for being intentional about his growth and development, when things got complicated, he would immediately go into flight mode. His attitude was these people have the problem, and they don't respect my intelligence or my skills. Charles has a difficult time taking responsibility for his lack of commitment to do a self inventory, commit to growth, dealing with difficult circumstances and people.

Charles had not become aware that he must take another level of responsibility and stop looking for convenience and realize that his mindset must be growth. Charles must start asking himself some questions about what is lacking in his professional development. What inventory of skills does he possess that he can use these challenges to develop a make him a more productive employee. How does Charles turn himself into more of an asset than a liability? As soon as he runs into difficult supervisors or issues relating to the job, the complaints start rolling in. They become excuses for being late, not showing up on time, learning to play by the rules, and make sure he tries not to cross a line that would put him into a position to get fired. Soon Charles will find himself in the same cycle in another job.

Key Takeaways

7

DON'T FIGHT THE PROCESS

The first impulse of the person hired is to determine what needs to change about the company more directly in the process. This way of thinking assumes that if the organization aligned with your level of understanding, it makes it comfortable for you to work and caters to your strengths. You may also think that somehow this organization would be a great place to work. This thinking is an immature posture to take because no system is made to conform to any one person. If this were the case, the organization would continuously function in the chaos, which causes it to cease to exist. In this case, no one would have an opportunity to increase value and raise their equity. Processes and systems are wonderful ways in which opportunities for growth, development, and increased equity are open to anyone on any level of entry into the organization.

> “ People who are of low self-value will find it very difficult to embrace the system. They will soon find out that the lack of self-value will limit their ability to grow and hinder the overall value of the organization. These are people who work for the check, live on the check, and live check-to-check. They bring the least amount of value to the organization based on their ability to see how the process and systems were created to give them opportunities to grow.

People with low self-value fail to invest in themselves; therefore, they have very little to invest in the organization. Their leadership IQ is very low, and they complain about leadership. They become expert critics on what leaders are doing, what they are doing wrong, or what they should be doing. The critics seem to have all the answers about how it should be done and yet they will not exert any energy in their self-development that can lead others and use their advice. Exerting the energy in their self-development, by the way, could be very beneficial to the progress of the organization.

Every system has its strengths and weaknesses, so do the people who work within those systems. Many times, people fail to see the fact that, as an organization has developed to a point where it now needs to hire many people so it can continue to grow and be profitable, it did not get to that point because nobody knew what they were doing. Entering into the culture of the organization and having success means that your opinion or thoughts about it don't matter. Coming into the organization, you should have had some idea of its culture. Doing your due diligence to understand as much as you can about the organization, its structure, strategy, mission, values, and history are all the responsibility of the person looking for a career opportunity. Those who approach the organization who don't take the initiative to do their proper research are probably not going to have much success if that gets into the organization. Waiting and depending on others to give you information, while they may be willing to do it, is not the best way to make sure you are prepared to be an asset to the organization. Those who will have greater success will seek to learn, understand, and fit into the structure and systems that already exist. They will make themselves avid students of the organization, ask the right questions, limit their input, and wait until they have been thoroughly immersed in the systems and culture. Before working to change what exists, it is essential to be careful to show that you respect and can function in what has already been established. Then, based on that knowledge and understanding, you can see how to add value and approach changes that may be necessary.

After several years, several jobs, and running into the same vicious cycle, Charles begins to stop looking for the problem in the organization and the supervisors and taking the time to do some soul searching about his commitment to himself first and then the organization. He begins to recognize that hopping around from job to job. Trying to start his own business thinking that if I were, the C.E.O things would be so much better than there was a much deeper problem that had to addressed and that problem was inside him. Once, he discovered that the first step in improving his self-value, personal equity, and leadership I Q was to own the fact that he didn't do the personal work for himself but instead considered that the role of the organization for which he worked. He realized that moving from organization to organization decreased his value and made him appear someone who could not be trusted or dependable. He begins to understand until he became stable, showed more significant levels of commitment, and work through problems to provide solutions; he would never get upward mobility.

Charles began to understand while education, intelligence, and skills are excellent, they must rest on a more profound commitment to do the real work of committing to personal growth.The willingness to change presumptions that are faulty and challenge his flawed mental models for the benefit of growth. Charles decides to return to the first organization he worked for and commit to the personal work on himself and improve his equity. A new era for Charles when he would find himself having opportunities that once eluded him.

Key Takeaways

8

WITH PROPER APPLICATIONS CHANGE AND GROWTH ARE INEVITABLE

I founded and have been the founder and president of a non-profit organization for more than thirty-four years. I have, like many other leaders of non-profits, dealt with and still deal with the day-to-day tasks needed to sustain a valuable and consistent organization that will serve generations to come. The challenges of the environment, building a healthy and sustainable culture, effect, and support the community.

Over the years, I have had the pleasure of working with some great people. One of the greatest joys in my life is seeing the consistent development and growth in the people around me. I continue to see lives change, witness the maturity and the development of gifts and talents, watch them evolve and do things, and accomplish great things, many of which they never expected to do when they became a part of the organization. People come and go, they move on, they take on new adventures, their lives take different trajectories, and it's a beautiful experience.

Two people that I want to reference still work with me today and assist me with my staff, my chief financial officer (CFO), and my administrative assistant. Both of them have been with me well over 25 years, and I am grateful for their continued support and service over the years. By the way, if I had to pay these two young ladies, I would need two more lifetimes for all that they have done and sacrificed to help us sustain to get where we are today. There are many volunteers who, without a doubt, keep us moving and support in ways that are awesome and so appreciated.

Both my CFO and administrative assistant joined me at very young ages early to mid-20s. All of us were very young and green if I might say, trying to feel our way in building an organization that would serve people and fulfill our mission. Both came with essential skills in the area in which they served, limited pay, but unlimited commitment and heart. As they begin to dig in and assist in the day-to-day operations, I began to see certain aspects of what human equity really looked like. While they had their specific roles and job descriptions, circumstances would arise time and time again, where they would have to be pulled out of their comfort zone and do things that they probably didn't like to do. Uncomfortable with the challenge, they, of course, dived right in. Many times, without warning, I stuck them in roles and gave them a task that had nothing to do with what they signed up for. The look in their faces when this happened was priceless, sometimes scary, but I figured it was 'do or die,' and we didn't have much choice — limited budget, a limited amount of people, and evolving families. Their consistent commitment, never complaining, always on task, still amazes me today. Many times I would feel guilty for putting so many responsibilities on them (don't tell them that). Yet, after a while, I began to see the principles of human equity, and leadership IQ began to work within their lives. These exercises helped them start to see the value that they really possessed far beyond some entry-level assistant and bookkeeper in the organization. They began to realize their value. They began to understand the many skills they had, and they started to see that they had significance far beyond what they were receiving in a check. They had the mindset that allowed them to recognize that engaging in the process, doing the uncomfortable things, taking on assignments that were totally outside of the scope of what they considered as skills and ability, increased their value equity and raised their leadership IQ in ways that can never be explained.

They found out that doing the uncomfortable things, taking on tasks that they might fail in, and doing the extra stuff that they may not have gotten paid for was not a loss. Still, it was a great source of expansion, professional development, growth mentally and emotionally, and it created an opportunity to increase their earning ability. Those things outside of the check allowed them to deal with weaknesses, raised their emotional intelligence, matured them to handle stressful situations, and the resolve to find a way to get it done. They never took the posture that they were being taken advantage of, or that they were being used. Instead, they took the posture or attitude, 'this is our investment.' They saw my sacrifice and investment, they watched me work and invest my time and effort in times when there was no financial benefit to me, and they modeled the same. They understood that real growth happens when they know their worth and that it is not indicated on a check, but in the wealth of skills, talent, and abilities that they were willing to invest. These types of investments are never losses, and the returns are unbelievable and will continue to come back with unlimited rewards and benefits.

Through this process, they were able to grow and

expand on many different levels, too many for me to put in this book. Both have developed skills that would quickly pay off if they opted to go into business and use some of the many talents to support others and help them both financially and administratively. They know how to start companies that they have seen and worked in every facet of business; their wealth of experience and expertise are very valuable in small business communities. There are so many needs that they can meet to include training, technical, social media and graphic arts support, accounting support, logistics, branding, childcare startup, and too many others to speak on. In any organization, it is useful when you have people who understand that they will benefit more than anyone else when they apply themselves to the process and systems that promote growth. The only limits on our ability to increase our value and develop leadership IQ are the ones that we place on ourselves when we don't comprehend those principles and processes that were put in place to build into us the transformation. We all need to grow. If the only value they saw were in the check, they would have aborted the process a long time ago. But because they recognized their value, were willing to invest their skills, gifts, and talents, the exponential growth and development in their lives is a reward in itself.

Key Takeaways

9

A COMMITMENT TO PERSONAL EQUITY

Raising personal equity and improving leadership IQ is about taking personal responsibility for growth. Personal responsibility requires self-discipline, staying focused on personal development, and taking the initiative to make investments for self-growth. The mindset for personal equity and leadership IQ requires an individual to take total responsibility for their development and resisting the need to hold the manager, company, organization, or anyone else responsible for personal growth and development. The first level of responsibility is to be accountable to one's self. There has to be a clear understanding that growth is about holding oneself responsible for the journey, process, and practices that make you willing to invest in yourself. Our first responsibility is to do what is necessary to stay balanced during times of stress, anxiety, fear, and other emotions. This requires time to invest in ourselves. If people are not willing to invest in themselves or make the needed sacrifices to achieve goals that will benefit their upward mobility, then why would anyone else invest and sacrifice their time to make sure they succeed.

Building personal equity and increasing leadership IQ is developed when an individual realizes that the person they must first lead is themselves. If people are good stewards over their own lives, then what will make them a good steward over others? This individual's work continues after work and begins before the actual workday starts. They do the little things, the extra stuff that will help them stay in pursuit of their dreams. They realize that ultimately they do nothing for free, even when money is not the immediate reward. It is an investment that they willingly make for their benefit and those whom they care for and love.

Charles had an awakening of sorts realizing that he'd been fortunate in gaining an opportunity, and it was up to him to seize it and soar with it. This attitude of appreciation and seeing his job and career as a way to improve himself, was a different approach for Charles. He began to appreciate the training he received, the lessons he learned, and his ability to face and learn from the tough challenges he experienced. Charles realized that he couldn't change others, and sometimes he'd have to deal with the hand he was dealt. He became excited about the work he is doing within himself to be a better employee. Charles committed to show the organization that he had value by being consistent, keeping an open mind, taking constructive criticism, and being fully engaged when working on a project.

Key Takeaways

10

COMMIT TO MAKING OTHERS BETTER

Making others better is the second step in our process that brings back great returns in our own lives. High leadership IQ requires that we have a responsibility to make others around us better because of the contribution we make to help them accomplish the assignment or project for which they are responsible. These people have to be highly motivated to work efficiently and effectively in ways that give their direct report confidence and willingness to reciprocate valuable information and training that will be of benefit to their growth. High leadership IQ requires that one has the interpersonal skills and emotional intelligence not to study the trade but to seek to understand the person for whom they are working. This is a skill that must be learned early as an entry-level employee. It will be one that will be much needed down the road when the employee moves to more responsibility, having persons that will soon answer to them for projects and work that needs to be done. Those skills needed may include understanding personality types, examining strengths and weaknesses that may exist, and understanding leadership style.s It is crucial that you make adjustments in your behavior that will fit in the culture of the organization, creating a happy medium for the most effective work relationship.

Proper assessment of yourself and others will help relationships flow better between leaders and subordinates. Ultimately, no matter what the weaknesses, flaws, or shortcomings of the leader, it is crucial that the employee work on sharpening his or her interpersonal skills. They must keep in mind that part of their future success will be determined by being able to work with difficult people in hostile environments. Making your supervisor, boss, or manager shine is vital in developing and growing leadership IQ. Leadership IQ is about making yourselves assets to those you work for, not liabilities. The more you work to make others successful, you position yourself to have more success. You earn the trust, confidence, and admiration of people who can count on you and appreciate the value that is added by you. Functioning this way opens the door for more excellent opportunities, promotions, and advancement on so many levels that will prove to reward your investment. This level of commitment to others will serve you well in many years to come as you leave a lasting impression on all those who cross your path.

Key Takeaways

11

THE BIG PICTURE

Keeping the bigger picture in mind, that whether in the organization you start in or some other organization, you will bring value and be valued based on the body of experiences, work, and accomplishments that will follow you to your next elevation and expertise. Your track record will be a testament to your value equity and your leadership IQ. Your level of growth achieved dealing with diverse cultures, environments, both good and bad, will be the foundation you need to ultimately achieve goals and dreams that at some point might have seemed to escape you. Many people lose focus on the big picture forgetting that the challenges they face every day will someday be assessed by someone who has a more excellent opportunity that awaits you. They don't realize that one day, someone will be looking to recruit, hire, and advance someone who has proven that they are worth more than they can ever be paid. The payoff can be amazing whether this person goes on up the corporate ladder or decides to take a leap and start their own company.

> "At the end of the day, it is essential to keep in mind that you will take with you every good and bad experience that helps to shape the leader you will become.

It will make you very valuable to any company or organization that is looking for the best of the best.

Leadership IQ requires that those working within the organization take the initiative to evaluate leadership models within the organization. It is beautiful to be motivated to take on more responsibility in leadership roles. Still, before making any real efforts to attain leadership positions, employees must take it upon themselves to understand that titles don't make great leaders. Ambition without the fundamental understanding of leadership will not contribute to higher leadership IQ. More specifically, the ability to observe and understand the leadership styles that are dominant within the culture of the organization. Employees should look for ways to examine what leaders do that brings particular success, those that seem not to be effective, and why this may be the case, not for reasons of being critical but for learning. How do individual leadership styles operate and function within the specific systems set into the organization? Is the leadership more top-down, or is it more rounded and based on team concepts where several people are tasked with and left to decide the direction of the departments? Would the employee prefer leading from a top-down perspective or facilitating teams that would lead the projects? Will they take more of a hands-on position when it comes to how projects are done, timelines, budgets, personnel? Becoming familiar with leadership theories and styles can give employees the edge in terms of being educated based on these leadership concepts. Remember that leadership IQ is the responsibility of the employee, not necessarily the organization.

Employees need to see leaders that model the practices and attitudes necessary to lead in the organization. This will usually require an investment on the part of the employee to volunteer and value the opportunities to the little things or extra things that raise their IQ.

> “Participating in additional curricular activities that most leaders are involved in will give employees access to

opportunities to mingle, talk to, and learn from those who can help them grow and develop.

So many employees miss out on the chance of promotion, growth, and development because they are not willing to go the extra mile and invest in themselves for the benefit of growth. They see these opportunities as unnecessary, and they don't have time, it doesn't pay any financial gain. This is why the average company or organization is having problems with the revolving door of turnover, tardiness, the lack of morale, and low production. Employees must know that with the right attitude and commitment to increasing leadership IQ and their equity, that organization is motivated to give them new levels of opportunity. Employees should be motivated to study systems within the organization, understand how they work, and offer up solutions that will improve the systems, make them more productive, saving the company money, and improving the quality of work life.

The values of the organization are at the heart of what makes an organization exceptional. Organizations need structure, but people need values. Values are the heartbeat of any organization, and without the heartbeat, the frame has no life, and people began to operate like robots. Leadership IQ requires that employees understand the values, the priority of values, and the need to do and work with those values in mind. When values have to be compromised to do the bottom-line work, meet sales quotas, and deadlines, it soon loses its way. Values are the compass that shows organization whether or not they are still on course, off a little, or totally in unfamiliar waters that threaten their very existence.

Personal equity partnered with leadership IQ is a powerful combination and a formula for continued growth and development in the context of an organization, whether it be nonprofit, corporate, military, or civil. Every individual that is employed or a part of an organization can themselves be no more significant in value to the organization than the value they place on themselves. The ingredients needed to make a successful organization lies in the human resources within it. Many are hidden under mindsets that cover them: self-value issues, limited belief systems about money, systems, and processes. If I don't place a value on myself, then I can be of no value to the organization to which I belong. The beginning of increased individual equity starts with the realization that you have something of value to offer beyond your job description, beyond just showing up to work and doing a job that you are paid to do. It means that once a person understands their value, they must have a mindset of being willing to invest, give, and volunteer. They realize that nothing they do is for free because the reward of their investment is far greater than the check they receive, just doing enough to get by. One concept that reinforces this idea is servant leadership. Servant leadership says that no matter where you are on the ladder of hierarchy, your greater responsibility is to serve those you lead, serve those on your level, and serve those that lead you. It is an all-around attitude of helping others.

Key Takeaways

12

SERVANT LEADERSHIP

The servant leadership model is a powerful way that everyone in the organization can maximize their efforts and choose purpose over ego. Every individual is committed to the good of the whole rather than the benefits of a few. Servant leadership reminds everyone that they are fortunate to have the opportunities provided them by having careers, to have better quality lives, to make a difference, to take care of their families and one another. The act of investing, participating in a process, and committing to observe and learn, produces growth. Leadership IQ is increased in the natural process of our commitment to one's development. The more your leadership IQ grows causes the continued development of your individual equity. Servant leadership emphasizes the core characteristics of a leader rather than technical skills, talents, or educational status.

They are:

1. Listening and Understanding
2. Acceptance and Empathy
3. Foresight
4. Healing
5. Conceptualizing
6. Persuasion
7. Building a sense of community
8. Stewardship
9. Awareness
10. Commitment to the growth of people

Servant leadership is transformational in nature, seeking to create motivation that is intrinsic based on how people connect out of influence due to relationships rather than focusing on the rewards for deeds done.

Greenleaf states, "A new moral principle is emerging, which holds that the only authority deserving one's allegiance is that which freely and knowingly granted by the led to the leader in response to, and in proportion to, the clearly evident servant stature of the leader" (Robert K. Greenleaf, 202, Pg. 23).

Real value and leadership IQ can only be developed when everyone in the organization can embrace the issues that are not results of some event, action, or reaction from others. Still, it is merely the failure to look within, hold ourselves accountable, ask ourselves some hard questions, and commit to action. It means that you can only hold ourselves responsible and nothing or nobody can stop your ability to increase value through equity and raise your leadership IQ. That choice belongs to you and you alone. Even if you feel unappreciated, slighted, mistreated, sabotaged, or even get laid off, when you know your value, equity, and that your IQ was developed, whatever you have gained will be a benefit to those organizations that need what you have become. Our job is to make sure it is their loss and not yours.

Key Takeaways

13

LEADING FOR THE LONG HAUL

There is a need for those in the workforce who are proactive, goal-oriented, and focused on the creation and implementation of a creative vision. Companies are looking for those who will elevate themselves by determining the direction, designing the organization, and nurturing a culture dedicated to excellence. Understanding this upfront will afford you the necessary attitudes and mindsets to assist the organization in accomplishing its mission. Organizations offer incentives to support your success, but you must have enough self-discipline to resist the need to make your quotas and your goal a priority at the expense of the well-being of the organization. Every day there will be easy ways to take short cuts, make the numbers look good, but must realize that instant gratification that looks proper short term will cost you dearly in the long run.

> Self-management and discipline is something that must be intentional and consistent in order to have long term success.

Being ethical in every contest is vital to longevity. You must be a person that makes integrity a priority. The impulse to compromise, get more for less, and take short cuts is powerful. You have to be committed to the long term rewards when keeping integrity in tack.

When onboarding with organizations, you must keep in mind that there are organizational barriers, in many cases, that you must overcome. The organization's systems, such as information systems, behavioral and political barriers, and those who are embedded in the status quo, may be faulty. In the status quo, you may have to deal with those who are content with the way things are. The adage is 'if it is not broke, don't fix it.' They are embedded in what works today, and they don't want to deal with problems and challenges of change. Many individuals don't like change and the risk necessary in making those changes. Systematic challenges are those that have to deal with information processing, reporting relationships that are in bureaucratic systems that impede communication because of rigid rules and procedures that will sometimes build resistance to change. Behavioral barriers are the result of biases and limited perspective, some of which are the result of education, training, and work experience. Political barriers arise from the power of relationships. Many times, this type of barrier is revealed in refusals to share information, conflicts over information resources, departments, and divisions, and even petty personal decisions.

If you plan to be exceptional in the organization, you must be willing and able to overcome barriers to change. One must understand the purpose and use of power within the organization.

> “There are four types of power within an organization: legitimate power, reward power, coercive power, and informative power.

Legitimate power, which is a power given within the context of the order and structure of the organization, is handed down by those who have the authority to do so. Reward power comes from positive behaviors or outcomes. Coercive power is the power manager exercises over employees using fear of punishment for errors of omission or commission. Informative power is the result of the manager's access, control, and distribution of information that is not freely available to everyone in the organization. As an effort to raise equity and leadership IQ, employees need to accept the fact that has to work to be innovated, producing innovative ideas and concepts that they are willing to share whether they are implemented or not. Lower and mid-level employees are always more likely to be motivated to bring forth new and innovative ideas; hopefully, they are in an organization that will be open to new ideas and concepts.

Key Takeaways

14

LEARNING THE ORGANIZATION

It is imperative to be conscious of the nature of the organization to which you belong. Some organizations are geared toward providing an environment conducive for learning, while others may be equipped to do what they are told and don't ask a lot of questions. In many cases, employees are not encouraged to ask questions but instead follow the script. In these cases, learning can very challenging. This system does not promote information sharing, adaptation, or decision-making. The employee is required to be clear about their intention to gather information, be more attentive, tap resources that give them more insight and be proactive in seeking out relationships with others that have the available information. The desire to develop personal equity and leadership IQ will be a motivating factor even in a difficult situation where communication and learning may not seem to be the priority. Many times, organizations can get so focused on the profits of the company and product that they fail to step back and consider whether or not the employees are growing and developing. Steven Covey uses the analogy of the goose that lays the golden eggs. The goose is the organization; the eggs are the reward for production. He points out that it is not a wise thing to neglect or kill the goose, trying to get more eggs. When you fail to nurture and take care of the goose, eventually, the goose gets sick, dies, and there is no more goose. Even worse, if the owner kills the goose to get to the eggs, the owner goes out of business.

When you are a part of a learning organization, cherish the opportunity and don't take it for granted. Being in a learning organization is the opportunity given to you. It puts you in a great environment to be creative with other opportunities to interact with people at different levels throughout the organization. Learning organizations are committed across the board to change, they are action-oriented, and they promote appropriate tools and methods that benefit everyone. Ken Melrose asserted, "I came to the understanding that you best lead by serving the needs of people. You don't do their jobs for them; you enable them to learn and progress on the job." In the article Organizational Dynamics, Robert Quinn and Gretchen

Spreitzer made an interesting point about two dramatically opposite perspectives on empowerment. In a top-down view, it is focused on delegation and accountability – senior management has to develop a clear vision and communicates the specific plans to the rest of the organization. This strategy of empowerment consists of the following:

- Start at the top
- Clarify the organization's mission, vision, and values
- Specify the task, roles, and rewards for employees
- Delegate responsibility
- Hold people responsible for results

On the other hand, the bottom-up approach will always have more risk associated with it. But for the benefit of growth, change, and giving people trust to do the right thing, it usually pays off. This strategy requires a high tolerance for failure and typically gives people a desire to buy in and ask for forgiveness rather than permission. The critical elements of the bottom-up position are:

- Start at the bottom understanding the need for empowerment

- Teach employees self-management skills and model behavior
- Build teams on encouraging corporate behavior
- Encourage intelligent risk-taking
- Trust people to perform

These two approaches are fundamental to most organizations. One strategy may be better in a particular context, and the other may work more effectively in another, especially while a small organization is growing and expanding. Employees need to be self-aware of how you function in either situation.

Key Takeaways

15

WORKFORCE TURNOVER

Turnover in the organization is a significant concern with baby boomers exiting the workforce in droves, and off to retirement. Many organizations are struggling to replace the individual equity and leadership IQ that has begun to move out. There are many theories as to why turnover is such a challenge in many organizations. A few of those theories are workplace environment, income concerns, conflicts in culture and behaviors in the workplace, and poor work performance. It could be a combination of two or more, but let's examine the issue of poor performance and a significant way that turnover is the result. In recent research, it suggests that an employee's job performance may influence job attitudes that ultimately end in turnover.

> Poor job performance almost always leads to poor positions in the workplace.

In many cases, poor performers try to rationalize their performance. Poor performance has also been shown to lead to increased anxiety and frustration (C. Cooper & Payne 1978); three studies have shown that poor performance represented a vital influence of voluntary turnover. (Marsh &Mannari 1977). Spencer & Steers, 1981. Wanous, Stump & Bedrosian, 1978. While there is only one perspective out of many others as to the source of turnover, it is a significant concern because it points back to mindset and attitudes that are seemingly at the root of many turnover issues in the organization. Other problems with turnover could be communication barriers, lack of morale, and limited upward mobility for promotion. Human equity and leadership IQ should, in these cases, be the overriding concern of the employees in the organization. The focus is on how employees adjust their attitudes in situations where the job may not be a good fit for them. For example, if a job does not pay enough, instead of focusing on the pay, they should turn their attention to the experience received, building a good history of consistent work, learning, and growing their own personal equity and leadership IQ.

This segment of your work life could be more

about building character, a stronger desire for personal improvement, and a more profound desire to learn. When these mindsets evolve in the workplace toward the organization, it is the result of growth in employees that get them in a position to see their income grow. Even if you don't desire to stay long with the organization, while you are there, practice a great attitude, excellent work ethic, be a great learner, be a better communicator and get as much value as you can out of the experience. Not all turnover is considered to be negative. There are a lot of positive results that can come from turnover; however, I am focusing on the need for the employee who will be in an ever-changing environment. Whether internally or externally, the employee must be aware of self, as well as the internal situation in which he or she may work, along with the external environments and the effects they may have on the organization and ultimately the individual.

People are continually moving in from organizations, and it is important to re-evaluate and asses the dynamics of the organization to ensure that whatever the reason for turnover, everyone in the organization is clear about their position and part in ever-changing circumstances. Many times, organizations will look to promote from inside to replace turnover. In this case, employees need to be mindful of opportunities that may arise and consistently prepare themselves to seize those opportunities. Organizations that do this may see a rise in morale because it is evident that new and fresh opportunities for promotion are available. Turnover at lower levels of the organization may not affect the organization in ways that turnover from higher levels will occur within it.

The level of skill, experience, talent, report with other critical stakeholders in the organization may be a difficult challenge for those who are responsible for replacing them. In organizations where demands are stringent, that may produce levels of stress and burnout over time, it is necessary to be cognoscente of the burnout factor and take preventative measures to keep the pressure limited or become overwhelming. This comes with a keen awareness of yourself and the environment you're in. Take advantage of the resources provided by the organization to help mitigate the level of stress and burnout you might experience. Once employees become cynical and critical, motivation to do the job at the level of excellence necessary will more than likely decline. Employees should be aware that training is a significant expense that companies have to deal with in getting new employees up to speed and ready to be profitable to the organization. Employees must be aware that some organizations will not bring you on based on how they interpret your ambition, and if they have confidence that you will stay on long enough to invest, they will make it worthwhile.

I want to suggest that you see yourself as an organization, a small micro-organization that has the same potential to enter an environment, grow in that environment, and become profitable so that you can serve the purpose of why you are present in the first place. All organizations should be focused on developing and having great success, being profitable, and serving the greater good of the community in which it exists. Focus on what you bring to the table, those tangible and intangible resources that add value to what projects you are engaged in. Just like a new business has to find its place in an environment that may have some level of resistance, as you enter into a new work environment you should be aware that you will also have to overcome some resistance. Once again, focus on what you bring to the table, both tangible and intangible resources that add value to whatever you are engaged in.

Just like a new business has to find its place in an environment that may have some level of resistance to your success in entering the new environment. While you may be greeted on the front lines with smiles and optimism that you will succeed in this organization, you will soon find out not everyone is on board with you being there. Human nature many times is as such that fellow employees are concerned about their job, keeping it safe, getting the job done, and getting home as soon as possible. You can't afford to sit back and wait for others to spoon feed you information, instruction, and training. Your competence can get you into the organization, but developing your capacity and turning your potential into an actual new level of expertise is always the goal. Ability speaks intrinsically to what you have that has not yet realized by you and those you work for. However, there is a knowing with the proper application of time and skills over time that you will see capacity grow into different levels of competence.

To stay on the path of building personal equity and leadership IQ requires that you put your heart and soul into accomplishing the task to which you have been assigned. You should create a mental model, designed in your mind, that will give you a clear mental picture of what you are to become and accomplish in this segment of your career and work life. A clear mental model of where you want to go will help you to get through times when things get tough or engaged in conflict, and ultimately trying to handle crises in an effective way. Having the right mental model for where you want to be in the future, with the organization or any other organization, requires that you learn to be comfortable being uncomfortable. You must see failures as practice for improvement.

Handle failure with the right attitude whenever you can stretch yourself and depend on others less, especially when it is within your scope to get it done. Be willing to think outside of the box. Always be prepared to entertain new concepts and ideas that might not match yours. Be ready to rethink and access further information that will allow you to be sharp and focused. Never be afraid to encourage others to challenge beliefs and old mindsets that they have adapted from past experiences.

Think critically about all aspects of those areas that concern and affect you. One exercise you can do is what I call the man/woman in the mirror. This exercise is to help you think differently about your commitment to higher personal equity.

The Man/Woman in the Mirror

Sit down and write 7 to 10 attributes that you admire and respect in a leader you know or desire to know.

After coming up with that list, stand in front of the mirror, and ask yourself how many of these attributes do you have.

Ask yourself: Is it fair to look for these attributes in others when you may not possess them yourself?

Acknowledge those attributes that you listed for that leader and see how many of your attributes match those of the leader. Doing this will give you time to reflect and determine what you see as weaknesses and strengths. This exercise will also show you what you need to focus on and develop in your personal development.

The extra mile principle is one I use to explain to people if you want to stand out and position yourself to have the recognition that comes from being diligent. Always consider going the extra mile whenever it is possible. If someone asks you to complete a task and they precisely identify what they desire of you, always try to give them more than they ask. Show your equity by going the extra step, getting more done than expected. Your leadership IQ will expand and reach new heights as you are intentional about wowing those who have assigned specific roles and responsibilities. Beat deadlines, try to do more with less, always exceed expectations, and work to bring the wow factor into play every day. Remember, the cream always rises to the top. Have a desire to be the best, never settle for mediocrity even if the work or job you do doesn't feel like it is of value. It is never the value in the position; it is your value that makes the difference. Remember, it is the difficult times that test us to determine what we really are made of. It takes courage to do the hard thing, rise above average, and be exceptional. There are times when you will hold your tongue even when you are right. There will be times when you will be mistreated, also taken for granted, but you must always keep the big picture in mind, keep your attention on ultimately what is going to benefit you. Don't allow your emotions to cloud your vision and cause you to lose your investment and the returns you deserve in life. Delayed gratification is something you must learn to have success and achieve your dreams in the future.

I remember a story a friend shared with me. He graduated from a particular field that dealt with agriculture. After he graduated, he began to seek out jobs and interviews with companies for which his skill set would match. I don't remember the exact details, but ultimately, he had an interview with a well-established company and interviewed for an upper management job. When he went to the interview, he was met with the vice president of the company. To his chagrin, the vice president was very rude and obnoxious, the interview was going south fast and in a hurry; ultimately, he knew he was not going to get the job. At some point in the interview, the vice president said, "The only thing you can do for me boy is gone and get me a watermelon." Infuriating the young interviewee, he got up and stormed out of the office, having a hard time handling his emotions because of the way he had been treated and spoken to. He explained that while riding to his next destination, he passed by a watermelon stand. At that moment, he was determined to take any action that resulted in him receiving a great job and getting an excellent salary to go along with it. He stopped, grabbed the watermelon, went back to the office, and delivered the watermelon to the man who had disrespected him. This act of overcoming adversity, thinking clearly about what he needed to do, and keeping his focus on the result that he wanted got him the position and the money he needed to make. As unusual as an incident like this was, maybe you, in some way, are faced with complicated people who, if you allow them to, will change our trajectory for where it is that you are striving to go in life. One split-second decision can launch you into the realization of your dreams or derail you, set you back, and make it that much more challenging to get to where you desire.

Your biggest challenges are not the challenges like the culture of the organization, the way the systems are running, the issues of training and support you receive, or the money that you make. Raising the equity and leadership IQ in your own life is where the hard work is. It's also in adjusting and changing your mindset, retooling the way you think about yourself, and what is really important to you. You are usually your worst enemy, and you hold yourself back with belief systems that don't promote progress and development. To know that you don't have to be stuck in old paradigms with limited thinking is, in itself, a great victory. Continue to believe that you have access to what you need to empower yourself so that you never see yourself at a disadvantage or as a victim of someone else.

> When you discover that tools, information, and knowledge is out there, and you are willing to put in the hard work on yourself, then the challenges you face in your organization will be minimal in comparison.

I often think about how many limited belief systems have been embedded in my mind and soul and how I allowed myself to be a victim of my own limited thinking. I am thankful for every opportunity to take back my personal power and work to change and make empowering strides to reframe my life. Hope is returned, faith is released, and new levels of freedom and joy are realized. Many times the way you see things is more of a problem than the problem you see. It is easy to come into an organization and assume that everything you think is wrong is wrong. Your way of projecting your attitudes and opinions into situations is based on the idea that you are right, based on the knowledge and information you have that may or may not be accurate. Steven Covey says,

> "The inside out approach says that private victories precede public victories, that making and keeping promises to ourselves precede making and keeping promises to others."

How can we think about this concerning the organization you work for. What promises are you willing to make to yourself first. What are you willing to promise yourself concerning how you want to see yourself as an employee? What are you willing to commit to for yourself in order to get the results you want? What are you willing to do to improve yourself every day to add value and be an asset? Are you willing to show up every day and show appreciation for the opportunity you have received to work, make a living, take care of your family, and prepare yourself for a great future? Anchoring yourself into commitments based on your vision, goals, and desire will position you automatically to get the best results out of your work experience and those resources that are available to you. Think about the attitude adjustments you need to make for your own benefit first. Be willing to question your attitude, its source, and the benefit it will be to you when working hard to accomplish those things that you are responsible for. Check your attitude at the door, be intentional about making corrections yourself. Doing this means you are proactively setting yourself up for progress and success regardless of what your day may bring.

> *Say to yourself, "I will have an attitude of gratitude for the job have. I will promise myself to respect those whom I answer too. I promise myself to be at work 30 minutes early. I promise myself to be a good steward over my time and resources."*

Real success comes from within when your own personal vision, desire, and purpose becomes what drives you. It will be in the painful experiences in your life when these desires will keep you anchored and on the right path. Personal vision and passion should be your compass when the environment is full of turbulence, and uncertainty is all around. When you find yourself in a hostile environment that does not support your advancement remember that the result is based on the decisions you make in your own best interest. Looking for others to support you, depending on them to fix the issues, change the culture to match you, or take time to make adjustments for your success causes you to operate from a place of dependency and not a position of power.

The most important person you have to impress is yourself. Creating habits that fundamentally align you with knowledge, skill, and desire are elements that you need to focus on because they together help to form habits that will help you be consistent in your behavior, no matter what the circumstances. To establish these habits, you first have to be open to receive knowledge to not only listen but listen deeply, not allowing your perceptions and preconceived ideas to be blocked. Allowing this will block new information about others, organizations, or jobs you may be required to learn or do. Steven Covey calls this habit "seek first to understand rather than to be understood." It is hard for people who always want to be understood first to open themselves up to understand. No matter what you think, you know you must be open to hearing what you don't know and improve your level of understanding. When you are open to learning and understanding through a desire to improve automatically, your skills will develop. This sets you on the path of empowering the mindset that you need to navigate to another level of growth and the maturity required to handle the level of success and responsibility you will receive.

Steven Covey says this concerning habits, "They move us progressively on a maturity continuum from dependence to independence to Interdependence." You determine how long you stay in each stage of the continuum by integrating these habits consistently and daily in your life. When you first start working in an organization, you may have to be more dependent than you may like to. No one wants to look like they don't have a clue, but seeking to understand, the desire to grow, and developing skill continues to move you toward the highest level of maturity and interdependence. Moving from dependence to independence is the second stage of growth necessary for you to move up the scale of maturity and a deep sense of personal achievement. Independence is the ability to work well, take responsibility, do what is needed to be done without relying heavily on anyone else, not needy, a self-starter, motivated, and willing to take the initiative. The final stage is interdependence. Interdependence is the desire and choice to work with others synergistically for better and more efficient results. You have to be intentional and secure about working with others with mutual respect and commitment to the objectives.

The conversations that we have, the language that we use is a definite reflection of mindsets and belief systems. The way we communicate with others is very important, but even more important, the bigger issues are the language and communication that you have with yourself. Many times, what you say publicly or what you give voice to is not aligned with conversations in the background that you are having with yourself. You may be saying one thing to your co-workers or supervisors, sharing with them what you have in confidence, you will meet the deadlines given, you will achieve the goals ahead. At the same time, there is another conversation you have with yourself, speaking to your doubts, fears, or lack of confidence. The good thing is, you have the ability to change the language, the self-talk that does not reflect what you really want to do and who you really want to be. Steven Covey shares with us the difference between reactive language and proactive language:

- **Reactive language:** There is nothing I can do; that's just the way I am. He makes me so mad. They won't allow that. I have to do that. I can't. I must. If only...

- **Proactive language:** Let's look at our alternatives. I can choose a different approach. I can control my own feelings. I can create an effective presentation. I will choose an appropriate response. I choose, I prefer, I will.

Many people are not consciously aware of the internal struggle with conversations that go on within themselves that may not have anything to do with their reality. The result of failure or shame in one's own life can create negative voices and languages that communicate something about them that brings them down, making it hard to function in different environments. Overcoming negative self-talk for many is a real challenge; being aware of what is taking place is half the battle. Negative self-talk has hindered, even paralyzed, many people emotionally. They have struggled to overcome and be intentional about overcoming this genuine obstacle. These negative conversations can lead to self-sabotage of one's own well-being. They can manifest themselves in procrastination and depression, and underestimate their ability to be effective in the workplace. Many times these dysfunctional conversations become excuses in the mind of an individual to give up, to quit, and turn to other vices they use to help them cope with this destructive mindset. In these cases, people will ultimately turn to some form of drug, alcohol, or addictive habits to cope. One solution is to deal with negative self-talk. Becoming aware of that negative self-talk is affecting how you see yourself and how you deal with others — taking time to become aware of how this internal language causes you to respond to job assignments and people to whom you are assigned to work with.

The good news is that self-talk can have significant positive effects as well. You can learn how to actively rescript your thinking by taking more new positive ways of thinking and interpreting feelings, redirecting them. Asking yourself the right questions will allow you to change your response to negative thoughts so you can stay focused and productive. Asking yourself if this is really what you feel or is this something others have caused you to believe. Where did these beliefs come from? How did they originate? Where is the evidence that any of this is true? Author Delvenia Fairbanks says, "Whatever self-judgment that is keeping you from your truth, you have the divine power within you to question its false core beliefs and replace them with new and better positive core beliefs that will bring happiness, peace, and reassurance of self-confidence and higher self-esteem" (pg. 18). Look at your past traumas or events that promoted a lot of fear and anxiety in your life. Start there and insert some empowering questions that will disarm those thoughts and beliefs that were birthed out of bad experiences. Remember, you have the right to manage your life, to change the things that hinder your evolution and growth. Experiences on the job may bring these issues up because of the need to truly be successful. Don't look at it as a negative experience when you have challenges that come from old faulty belief systems. Look at it as an opportunity to work to find a solution, overcome it, and become better in the areas you struggled with. You are not by yourself; everyone has some area of their life that they are working to correct if they want to go further in life. You are not alone, so don't resist talking to others and having those meaningful conversations you need to have in order to resolve the issues. Talk to a counselor, a trusted friend who knows you, a pastor, or a spiritual leader who may be able to help you in your journey to be your best most powerful self.

Key Takeaways

16

CHOOSE TODAY

No matter where you might be as it relates to your career, job function, or position in life, whenever you choose when it is time to up the ante, it's yours for the taking. There are no limitations; there is no ceiling, only the ones you put on yourself because of external and internal conditions that you always have the ability to overcome and proceed to where you want to be in life.

> No matter how far you have come or what you have achieved, there is always more that you can accomplish and heights you can rise to if you dare to do so.

The first thing you need to do is evaluate your goals, look at what you have done to get this point, and see if they are still relevant to taking you where you need to go. Maybe you might have to prioritize your goals differently. You might have to delete goals that are not supporting what you want to achieve and create a new list of goals that better fit where you see yourself in the next 5 to 10 years. Goals that support a five to ten-year vision will keep you aligned and moving in the right direction.

Set very clear and specific goals, try to eliminate those vague and general goals that don't tie you to specific things you have to do. Give yourself crystal clear steps in reaching these concrete goals that help you move closer to where you need to be. Be sure to look at the obstacles that could lay ahead; what will you have to overcome in order to get to your goal. Take the time to plan a strategy that will help you proactively go through scenarios in your mind and how you might address them for the outcomes you want. Many times, the ability to use vision to see possible threats and obstacles will allow you also to envision what your solution is to deal with those barriers. Be realistic about your timelines, and when you will be able to work on your goals. Prepare yourself to deal with some of the issues that may arise on the way. Establish a timeline, block out space in your calendar for specific work you are going to engage in your steps for preparation. The fact that you are clear about what you want will compel you to make time, make sacrifices, get support from those closest to you, and keep you motivated to see it through. Having these timelines and benchmarks will help you become better at time management. It will help you stay clear about the priorities on your journey and stay away from time killers, overcome procrastination, and still have time for other things that you need to take care of. When you find yourself in a rut, or when unexpected things take place that brings stress, you will know that your consistent commitment to your vision and goals will motivate you to get back on track. When setting up timelines or looking at deadlines, take into consideration that you have a built-in cushion for the unforeseen circumstances that will pop up. Often when a contractor bids on a job, they always build in the budget resources for unseen issues that will arise so that they don't go over the budget and lose money. When planning, make sure to do the same way. When the unforeseen pops up, generally you will not stress, you are somewhat prepared for it because you factored it in from the beginning.

Always be aware of where you are concerning the goal you set out to achieve. Being mindful requires self-management and discipline. Many times, good meaning people can put pressure on you because they don't understand what your mission and goals are.

Avoiding temptations to attend events, trips, and other extracurricular activities will be difficult. You may not always resist, but again, factoring them into your timeline will help you stay on course. No need to beat yourself up, just keep moving forward.

Set review times into your timelines that will remind you that it's time to assess what you have accomplished and how far you have to go. Have confidence and faith that you will succeed, but know that it will not be easy. Work effectively, but make sure to have the mindset that you have to earn what you desire to achieve. Understanding that journey will be well worth it.

> “Have people around you that love you and support your goals and dreams. These are people who will hold you accountable for what it is you set out to do. You need people in our lives who will hold your feet to the fire and not let you back down when you desire to do so — people who are honestly committed to seeing you succeed and want the very best for you.

A desire to be better is clearly a great way to approach the goals that you want to achieve. While many people consider themselves as good, most don't see the need to be better. If you're going to rise and stay on the cutting edge, your core desire should be, I want to better. In contrast, it's ok to have healthy competition, wanting to be better than others. The best person to compete with is yourself, always trying to be better today than yesterday. If you keep your focus on being better, what the competition does isn't your primary concern.

I learned this a long time ago while playing golf: the only person I'm really competing against is myself because it is not fundamentally a team sport. I had to quickly realize, when you worry about everyone else's shot or score, yours usually goes up, and the result is not good. I have to focus on my shot, keeping my eye on the ball, learning how to leave bad shots behind me and try not to carry the last bad experience forward to the next shot. Often, we call it getting into someone's head. This is when you let others affect your thinking, throw you off, and cause you to make bad shots. It is often funny when the guys that practice the less and fail to work on becoming better are always upset when they don't achieve their goal to win, and others do so much better than they do. You have to realize in life that basically, it is you and the course, you may never beat the course, but it will only be as a result that you didn't do enough to better yourself.

I believe that all of us have so many resources,

equity, and potential to build our leadership IQ. We all must be aware that no matter how it looks, where we are in our life, career, or organization, we have the resources within us to continue growing, achieving, and accomplishing our goals and dreams. Remember that obstacles and challenges will only bring out the best in you when at your core, you believe in yourself, you believe that you have so much more value and that achieving your goals is within your power. Although my focus was mainly on your mindset and personal development within the workplace, many of these principles and practices can be used in any facet of life.

Charles began contemplating how he could increase his leadership IQ, and became proactive and in taking the initiative to find opportunities to add value. He decided to take advantage of his career opportunity and make personal investments that were not just for the dollar or benefits rather how he could contribute to the improvement of himself and his organization. He took the initiative to engage with his supervisors, ask questions, understand his assignments, and the philosophy behind the strategy implemented by his supervisors. Volunteering, he made himself available for events that supported the organization's community involvement. He begins to see initiative ways to help his colleagues and his team streamline and be more effective in meeting deadlines and improving the overall productivity of his team. He begins attending free classes in his off time that were relative to his job. He spent extra time in the library reading and understanding organizational dynamics, finding out ways he could better understand his organization's culture and practices. This commitment to his personal growth has paid in big dividends both for Charles and the organization he works for. Not long after this change in mindset and dedication to increasing his private equity Charles began to get the attention of his superiors, he became the topic of discussion in management meetings and soon received a significant promotion. Charles didn't stop there; he went back to grad school to get his masters and continued to work diligently to improve the quality of work-life for himself and others. Eventually, he received another promotion with significantly more money and benefits.

What happened? It's simple Charles realigned his mindset, chose to see the value he possessed and then invested it in the organization that gave him the opportunity. Not a whole lot has changed in the dynamics of the organization, but he made the decisive shift that has begun to put him on a trajectory the will take him afar as he desires to go.

Many times while coaching this young man, I had to question whether or not he was listening to anything I said. What a thrill to see him apply the technics and knowledge we shared and see him excel in such an impressive fashion. The beautiful thing about this is experience is that it doesn't matter who you are and where you can have the same results if they are open to shifting and reframing their mindset. Talent acquisition was a big deal when onboarding qualified people who will support the organization's vision and mission but, more importantly, is mindset acquisition the foundation for high productivity. Skillsets are teachable, information can are teachable, but the mindset is something that must be changed and intentional.

Key Takeaways

SCHEDULE A WORKSHOP

This book can be ordered in bulk for organizations and is supported by a comprehensive workbook that is made available exclusively in live workshop settings facilitated by the author. Please contact us at hawkinssolutions.org to get more information on having Felton Hawkins facilitate a workshop for your corporate, private, or non-profit organizations.

ABOUT THE AUTHOR

Felton Hawkins is the Founder of the Full Gospel Kingdom Church, where he has pastored for over 34 years. He has also founded Full Gospel Kingdom Churches, a network of Churches and pastors that he assists in developing and shaping their organizations. Felton earned a bachelor of arts degree in religious studies from Hampton University, a Master of Arts in organizational leadership from Regent University and an Honorary Doctorate from Providence Bible College and theological seminary.

Felton has spent over 34 years developing organizations, training leaders, consulting, and coaching leaders both nationally and internationally. His travels and expertise have taken him both nationally and globally to Cote D' Ivoire West Africa, South Africa, and Canada. Felton has committed to building and equipping everyone to tap into the leader and untapped resources that reside in them.

Teaching from his signature program, Leadership Equity Value Practices, Felton addresses the mindset and the approaches to self-development that break barriers and helps overcome the issues of mediocrity. These programs prove to be useful both in the nonprofit and corporate organizations, exposing the power of universal principles and how they can operate in anyone's life to lift them to achieve their dreams, even in the most challenging times.

Felton understands that there is no barrier or ceiling that can keep those who inspire to reach unlimited heights in their life from obtaining their goals. He resides in Hampton Va, with his wife Jasanta and six children.

ALSO BY FELTON HAWKINS

Developing Christians for Leadership

Building A Great House

Book 3

Printed in Great Britain
by Amazon

31528402R00064